The Undiscovered Jewel

Realizing the Brilliance that Lies Within

The Undiscovered Jewel

Realizing the Brilliance that Lies Within

Dell Scott

THREEFOLD PUBLISHING

The Undiscovered Jewel, Realizing The Brilliance That Lies Within
Copyright © June 2014
By Dell Scott

Published in the United States of America by Threefold Publishing

www.threefoldpublishing.com

Cover Design- Visual Lightning Graphic Design
Editing, Layout- Division of Threefold Publishing

All rights reserved under International Copyright Law. Contents and/or cover may not be reproduced, distributed, or transmitted in any form or by any means or stored in a database or retrieval system, without the prior written consent of the publisher and/or author. Unless otherwise noted, Scripture quotations marked KJV are from the King James Version Bible,© Copyright 2010, Zondervan, LLC. Scripture quotations marked NIV are from the New International Version Bible,© Copyright 2010, Zondervan, LLC.

ISBN: 978-1-63068-696-3
First Edition Printing
Printed in the United States of America

This book is dedicated to God, who created me in his image, which is excellence, my Mother who always told me how beautiful I was, my Father who always pushed me to display my brilliance, my Husband who always treats me like a precious gem, and my Children who are the diamonds in my life.

INTRODUCTION..9

CUT..13

COLOR...25

CLARITY..35

CARAT WEIGHT..45

COPYCAT 57

CARE...67

CLOSURE...75

SCRIPTURES 83

ABOUT THE AUTHOR..89

SOURCES..91

Introduction

Diamonds are gems of old, originating back over 3 billion years ago. They have been adorned by kings and queens, visualized as great wealth, and used to symbolize the everlasting covenant between husband and wife.

It is interesting to know that the origin of the word diamond comes from the Greek word "Adamas", which means unconquerable and indestructible. It is even more amazing to know that Adam, God's first created being was named from that same Greek root word meaning diamond. It is truly evident that all things created by God reflect brilliance and excellence!

Through this book, it is my desire, to take you on a journey to reveal the honest truth that ...YOU ARE A DIAMOND! In order to provide you with a clear understanding of this truth, I must walk you through the exhausting process that a diamond travels, to become that perfect gem.

It is estimated that it takes 1750 tons of earth to be moved, in order to find a one 1-carat "gem quality" diamond. Diamonds are formed deep within the earth's surface through a very arduous process. The process is a unique combination of high temperature and high pressure. The weight of the underlying rock bearing downward, mixed with the hot temperature of the area, forms carbon atoms. Through this hard bonding action, the carbon atoms lock into place and begin to form large crystals which create the diamonds we have come to treasure.

Even after the diamond is located in its raw state, it must go through additional man-made processes before it can reach its finished state. It has to be cut, it is sometimes colored or altered in appearance, it possesses its own internal flaws, and naturally it has its own weight. Well believe it or not, after you were created by God, you were allowed to go through similar processes to create the polished gem you were destined to become. You have been cut, you have some internal flaws, you have your own unique color, and naturally you have your own weight to bare in this walk called life. Due to the diamond-like process that God created you with, you have the resilience to go through trials and shine while doing it.

When you are finished reading this book, It is my desire for you to receive the same revelation that God gave to me... to know that your preciousness is comparable to that of a diamond. You were formed through a unique process with unmatchable brilliance.

Just like diamonds, you possess the 4 C's: A specific cut, a unique color, a rare clarity, and a specific carat weight. There are no two diamonds that are created alike and there is no other person on this earth that is created in your likeness. God went to great lengths to fashion you with specific qualities and attributes. He is waiting to uncover you, in order to reveal the spectacular gem you are to the entire world!

Cut

A diamond in its original form is just a dark, discolored and ordinary stone. It is buried and hidden far beneath the earth, before it is transformed into a sparkling gem through the cutting process. Out of all of the factors of a diamond, the cut is the most complex and technologically difficult aspect to analyze. At first thought, we think of a diamond's cut referring to its shape, but it actually pertains to how well a diamond's facets (flat surfaces) interact with light.

We all know there are different shapes that diamonds are formed into, such as round, emerald, pear, oval, and marquise. Each shape has its own unique cutting process it must endure to be created. God has done the same with us, we are cut or formed in different ways and we must all go through different processes in order to be used for his glory. Sometimes we look at other people's lives and envy the way their life sparkles and shines, but we do not know what cuts (trials) they have endured to arrive where they are at in life. The more a diamond is cut, the more facets it contains in order for light to be reflected. Like the diamond, we have all been fashioned to reflect light. That light reflects a part of the Holy Spirit moving inside of us, which ultimately reflects Jesus.

Basically, the more we are cut, the more that Jesus is seen operating in our lives. For example, an asscher cut diamond, has tremendous luster and a "hall of mirrors" effect whereas a cushion cut diamond has a range of spectral colors that are reflected. Both are brilliant cuts, but they reflect light in a different manner.

The facets of a diamond are the flat surfaces that we see cut into the diamond. They are commonly cut into a diamond in order to improve the appearance, by allowing the gem to reflect more light. God uses a similar approach and without "faceting" us, it would be impossible for his presence to be seen. God ultimately allows us to be cut by our trials, so that his light can reflect through us for all of the world to see!

The journey a diamond takes to reach the cutting process is truly amazing. It is composed supernaturally in the earth and then cut to perfection after it has risen to the surface. Jesus followed a identical course. He was pierced on the cross, he bled for the glory of God, and for our salvation. He was cut in the natural by man and then arose to be polished in the supernatural power of God, with the brilliance of the Holy Spirit.

It is exactly the same for us, only when we have been cut, can we be prepped for an awesome transformation like Jesus. The scripture, 2 Corinthians 1:5 (KJV) rings true, *"For as the sufferings of Christ abound in us, so our consolation also aboundeth by Christ"*. We must accept that being made in God's image, we are required to follow the same course as his son. For example, you might have lost a loved one to violence, but through that experience you purposed to open a foundation to help those currently enduring violent relationships. So being made in his image, we can take comfort in knowing that after enduring the process we receive God's power and shine more brightly than before!

The most amazing factor about a diamond's cut, is that the cutting process is crucial to its final beauty and value. The cutting of the gem actually gets the diamond closer to the final step in the finishing process, in which there is shedding of the unusable pieces. Look at how powerful that is! After Jesus had been cut, he shed his blood and proclaimed his father's will. His vulnerability to the power of sin, death, and the grave was taken away and he was resurrected with all power.

The Father wants us to have the same victory as his son and the same power after we go through our "cutting process". God wants to cut away at our iniquities and flesh-like tendencies, by allowing us to go through challenges where he can pour into us. He has to cut us to be able to pour into us, in order to reflect more of him. We ultimately reflect him by way of our testimony, which is our cutting process.

The effect of cutting diamonds, is a major factor that attributes to the characteristics that the gemstone will represent. The more faceted, the diamond, (meaning the more angles a diamond has) the more complexity the jewel will have. For example, an emerald cut, has the fewest facets of all, therefore it reflects less light. We are just as complex, in our individual nature as well. Just like a diamond is faceted to improve its appearance, God facets us or rather cuts us in a particular way, so certain characteristics that he has embedded in us can shine through.

I look at the situations that I have been through, that have cut me to enable me to become more humble, less prideful, more thankful, more loving, and more patient. I was being filled with traits that reflect the nature of God's son, Jesus Christ. Ultimately, God's goal is that when the world sees your many facets (traits), they will see him represented on each of them.

When a gemologist inspects a diamond, he sees the many angles of a diamond and might even see some flaws. However, when he turns the diamond from side to side, light is reflected off of the facets that have been cut into the gem and the brilliance of the gem is noticed. So when you turn from side to side, people should see love, they should see gentleness, and they should see faithfulness. They should see all the luminous aspects of Christ being reflected through you and around you!

Trained diamond cutters evaluate diamonds, by their original shape, weight, and color in order to determine the shape they should be cut into. Diamond cutting is a long and complicated process, so the cutter must be very cautious. The end result is to retain the stone's maximum natural weight, along with removal of inclusions or flaws, while increasing value.

That is the same process that God wants to take us through. He is our trained diamond cutter. Isaiah 64:8 (KJV) says, *"But now, O Lord, thou art our father, we are the clay, and thou our potter, and we all are the work of thy hand"*. Because the father fashioned you, only he knows what trials you must endure to be shaped and molded into that priceless gem. Like a gemologist with a trained eye, he knows what stage of the cutting process you are at.

There are 5 stages a diamond must go through before its process is complete: 1. Planning stage, 2. Cleaving stage, 3. Sawing/Bruiting stage, 4. Polish/Brillianteering stage, and 5. the Approval stage.

The different stages of a diamond can also correlate to where one is spiritually in their life. For example, the Planning stage; a new babe in Christ, the Cleaving stage; the separation or wilderness period, the Sawing and Bruiting stage; the cutting process (where you experience the trials), the Polishing/Brillianteering stage; the fine tuning period, or the final stage; which is fittingly named Approval. The Approval stage is where you have been pronounced qualified and tried by the fire! God knows what stage you are at and if you are ready to go on to the next stage. He wants to allow you to go through trials in order to be cut, not to diminish your value, but ultimately to increase your value for his glory.

As I recall the story of Job, like a gem, he was perfect and upright in God's eyes, but he had to endure an unimaginable trial. His sons and daughters were taken by fire, his cattle, and servants were killed; on top of being stricken with sickness. He had done nothing wrong to deserve this plight and he was even told by his own wife to "Curse God and Die!" He refused to do it and went through his cutting process. If you know the full story, only God the creator, could allow for Job to be cut. Did you know that it takes a diamond to cut a diamond? A diamond bladed saw is used to break a diamond into the desired shape. How befitting that we are made in his image and the great "I AM" is the only one that can mold us into the vessel of greatness that we are to become! The beauty of the story of Job is that he was blessed with more land, offspring, and wealth than he possessed before.

Just like Job, you have to be cautious that you do not allow anyone or even yourself to talk you out of your cutting process. Naturally those who care about us, do not want to see us hurt or in pain. But, there are some people who do not want to see the greatness in you ever come to fruition. They would rather talk you out of and walk you out of your destiny.

We have become a society that desires the prize but despises the process. Every possible shortcut is being preached and taught on how to become wealthy and successful. I assure you there is NO SHORTCUT. As a precious jewel, you have been predestined to take a certain path to reach the full potential of who you are called to be. Remember, I mentioned that the cutting process is the most complex out of all the 4 C's, so there is no way to attain immense fame and fortune if one does not go through their predestined trials and tribulations.

I have personally experienced trials where I tried to talk myself out of completing the process. In my mind and my heart, it would have been so much easier to walk away than to deal with a situation. I had a blended family dynamic where my husband and I could not see eye to eye. It felt like we were taking sides instead of standing side by side.

There were times when the issues became physically and mentally stressful. The more I wanted the drama to stop, the more it kept coming. I felt alone with no one to turn to and no one that could understand how I felt. I WANTED OUT! But I stayed... only for God to work the situation out on everyone's behalf. Through my trials, GOD was pruning me to first and foremost place my ultimate faith in him and secondly to be able to yield to him. Little did I know, he was working on those things inside of me that I lacked. He showed me how to have patience to wait on him and to place my faith in him because there was no one else to turn to. He was cutting away at issues that had been embedded in me for a long time. I am a very analytical person. So I have been always able to take a scenario and finagle my way around obstacles or challenges.

Well he brought me to a place where "I" and all of my intelligence, craftiness, and creativity was not in a position to do anything. People who were resources and shoulders to cry on were no longer available. God basically said, *"You have no choice but to seek me and wait on me because I am the only source you have, not your husband, not your friends, not your career, not even your beauty"*. He said *"Only I can fix your situation, Only I can fix YOU"*. God knew how to cut me perfectly in order to get what he needed OUT of me in order to put what he needed INTO me.

A diamond must be cut perfectly as well. It has to be cut to the right depth for maximum light reflection. If the cut is too shallow or not deep enough, then the light reflection will be hindered. Remember I said, that we all have to be to be cut differently therefore we all have to go through different processes.

In addition to the process he was taking me through in my family dynamic, he also cut me by allowing me to see my reflection in my children; those most precious to me. He used my "precious gems" to reflect the very things that I was challenged with. He used my daughter and son to reflect my lack of patience, my selfishness, my quick temper, and the imbalance in my life. He knew exactly what I needed to see.

The reality is, dealing with my process was hurtful and painful. He left me in a position where there was nothing but him. God knew what it took to get me to yield. Sometimes God will isolate you from everything you hold dear, not because he doesn't love you, but because his wisdom knows what he has to pour into you and pull out of you, to prepare you for ultimate greatness!

Even Jesus had to go through isolation, even he had to be cut, even he had a moment where he wished his process would be over. In the end, he said, *"Nevertheless, not my will, but thine, be done"* (Luke 22:42 KJV).

If it is any consolation, know that WE ALL MUST GO THROUGH. By the blood of Jesus, we are made more perfect in God. The only decision we can make is to choose HOW we go through our process. Paul said, in James 1:2-4 (NIV), *"Consider it pure joy, my brothers and sisters, whenever you face trials of many kinds, because you know that the testing of your faith produces perseverance. Let perseverance finish its work so that you may be mature and complete, not lacking anything"*.

So embrace your process to greatness, count it all joy that God considers you to be precious like a diamond in his eyes. Let him finish the work he has begun in you, making you lack nothing and being complete in everything!

Color

As there are no two snowflakes alike, every diamond is a miracle of time, placement, and chance. God made us in different shapes, sizes and colors and we are also radiant in our own way. I have come to the realization that many of us find difficulty in accepting how God has physically created us. Society would have us to believe that we have to look a certain way to have value or status, but find joy in the fact, that our creator placed a very specific value inside of us when he formed us.

Similar to the way color produces different sensations to one's focal point (as a result of how an object emits light), so does the color or brilliance he placed inside of you affect the way you reflect to the world. The same way we are formed in various shades, features, and colors, diamonds are fashioned in the same manner.

Nature occasionally produces diamonds with naturally occurring blue, brown, pink, deep yellow, or even green hues. The amazing thing about this fact, is the geographical conditions required to yield these colors are truly rare.

Those rare conditions make these diamonds with distinct and naturally occurring shades scarce and highly prized. This is exactly how and why God made YOU completely different from anyone else. So if you don't fit society's standards, know that God took great care in using priceless materials in creating you. There is no one on earth like you! You can't be physically duplicated or recreated! You are priceless, rare, and brilliant!

In my profession as a stylist, I assist women who want fashion makeovers. As I consult with these women, it is often necessary to discuss sensitive areas of a physical nature. I meet with women who do not like their body, their hair, their nose, their complexion and the list goes on. Because of what I have been through, God has given me a keen ability, known as discernment in these areas to be able to identify and relate to the issues. For those that he sends my way, I usually find that the desire for change stems from an issue of self love. He allows me to see the luster in their "color" is dulled not by the physical attributes they seek to fix, but by the inner brilliance they do not see within themselves.

Believe me, I know what it's like to not embrace who you are, to feel like you are not beautiful because something about you does not fit the norm. I wanted to be a runway model, so I went through a period where I regretted not being taller. I went through a phase where I wanted my nose to be more keen. I even had a period in my younger years where I planned to alter my appearance, after I graduated from high school. Sounds crazy, right? Even though you might not verbalize it, we ALL have went through a phase where we did not like something about ourselves. The sad truth... is that some of us still do.

We as women, need to realize that we are like those rare, colored diamonds. Even colored diamonds, despite their rarity, have some flaws and imperfections, but nonetheless they are still priceless. It has been recorded that a blue diamond fetched 24 million dollars at an auction and a vivid pink diamond was sold for 10.8 million dollars. So I dare say, what is considered to out of the norm is highly prized. Still, you might say, I prefer a diamond that is white over a colored diamond, but keep in mind that color has special meaning biblically. Over and over again, the bible uses the significance of color as well as the significance of gems.

For example, Amber symbolizes God's glory and brightness, Green represents life, Blue symbolizes heavenly things, and Crimson represents the covering, the blood. Even when you do not look like other gems, you are still precious, because you have your own distinct value.

Certain colored gems were used in constructing decorum for priests, kings, and buildings of God. It is said, kings wearing breastplates with diamonds were revered in battle, and only officials titled in high esteem wore precious jewels. In the City of God, the 12 foundations of the wall were garnished with specific stones in a specific order as God had instructed. I am sure that he strategically placed each gem in the wall, according to its composition, color and symbolism.

We serve a very specific God, HE used certain people for certain tasks in the bible for a reason. HE distinctively "colored" you not just in complexion, but in complexity. You were created or colored in a particular way to be able to impact certain people in certain arenas that others will not be able to. HE knew exactly how you needed to be fashioned, from every hair on your head, to your features, and even your complexion.

We need to see that we are all unique. We might all have different complexions, shapes, and features, but we were all made in the image of the creator. Some of the most beautiful women in the world have many cultures influencing their ethnic origin. I want you to know that whatever your ethnic background, whatever your skin tone or whatever unique feature you possess, you are beautiful and stunning just like that colored diamond!

This is why you have to embrace who YOU ARE! Sometimes we have what I call an "identity crisis" in the natural and in the spirit. We try to enhance our physical being to cover up or erase who God has created us to be. Society would have you to believe you need medical procedures to *completely* alter yourself or your features, but rest assured when God made you, he "colored" you exactly as he wanted you!

The definition of the word color, used as a verb, means: to change the color or appearance of something by painting or dyeing it. The devil, who is the wickedness of this world, wants to convince you to "color" yourself in a way physically that would spiritually misrepresent God. He wants you to believe that God made a mistake when he created you. He wants you to use worldly devices to alter the very brilliance that God has placed inside of you.

I want you to know that very mindset is a lie! God predetermined your "makeup" when you were in the womb and he does not make mistakes. Just as there are physical enhancements used in the world, there are similar coloring enhancements used on diamonds. A process called "coating" masks an undesirable body color with an ultra thin layer of chemical or plastic. Another form of coating involves applying a thin film of synthetic diamond to the surface of a diamond simulant to give it similar characteristics of a real diamond. These techniques may hide or cover things people deem as being "undesirable" in a diamond, just like we do in our natural being.

Be mindful, when you start to make enhancements and alterations to your physical being, it may affect your brilliance. Have you ever recalled a celebrity that had plastic surgery, but actually looked better before rather than after? You become focused on the enhancements they had done versus what actually drew you to them in the first place. There are well known actors that had surgery and their demand in their industry declined because of it.

What they thought they needed to feel better about themselves or to be more successful, actually removed some of the brilliance they possessed. This is why I can't stress enough that you have to begin to embrace and love who you truly are. Some alterations we have done to ourselves can cause permanent damage and affect the value that we possess. Your radiance was paid with a price. Only when you possess your full value can the glory of God be revealed.

HPHT is a high pressure, high temperature process that changes the color of certain diamonds to make them colorless. Similarly, God uses the pressure of our experiences to draw us into him. He does this in order to change our "color" to make us look more like him. During our spiritual journey, as we start to decrease fulfilling our desires and increase fulfilling God's desires, others start to see more of the great "I AM" than of our own likeness.

The more we strive to be like him, the more of his Holy Spirit we possess. The more of the Holy Spirit we possess, the more people see the Christ in us and less of ourselves. The more absent of our own color we become, the more we "color" ourselves in his image. Consider this, being in Christ reflects no specific color, race, creed or origin, like society labels us to be. When we become "colorless", we are walking in the full power of his Holy Spirit. Believe it or not, the color evaluation for most gem-quality diamonds is based on the absence of color.

It is stated that a chemically pure and structurally perfect diamond has no hue, that's right no hue! Just like a drop of pure water it consequently, possesses a higher value. When we start to mirror Christ, we start to possess a higher value like that structurally perfect gem. Christ is the ultimate diamond... full of color yet as perfect as a colorless jewel!

Clarity

Clarity can refer to physical characteristics in a diamond, but it can also refer to state of mind, point of view, or physical characteristics in an individual. Clarity in diamonds can be affected by carbon being exposed to tremendous heat and pressure deep within the earth.

This process can result in a variety of internal characteristics called "inclusions" and external characteristics called "blemishes". A diamond's clarity refers to the absence of those inclusions and blemishes.

Evaluating the clarity of a gem is a process that determines the number, size, nature, and position of these said characteristics; in addition to how they affect the overall appearance of the gemstone.

Our clarity as an individual is evaluated or affected in the same way. Psalm 51:5 (KJV) says, *"Behold I was shapen in iniquity; and in sin did my mother conceive me"*. We were born with certain issues and flaws just like a diamond. Some of our flaws are like inclusions, embedded deep, unnoticeable to the naked eye, while others are like blemishes more easily seen by others.

Clarity also deals with how others perceive us and how we perceive ourselves. It is human nature to be concerned with how other people view us. The truth is most of us know what our issues or concerns are; be it external or internal. We do not want others to know so we try to conceal the truth, but like a precious jewel our flaws become more visible through magnification. Unfortunately, we have become more concerned with society's perception of us than what we actually think of ourselves. It could be as simple as thinking that our physical features are not what society dictates as being beautiful.

Ask me how I know. I recall having been asked to visit and minister to one of my sister's in my church. When I arrived at her home, she was very distraught. As I am tried to calm her down, she said to me,

"You don't understand, you have it all together". I said, "Look no one has it all together, my issues might not be your issues and your issues might not be my issues, but we are all dealing with something." We were able to talk at length and she began to feel better about her situation. The moral of this story is that we are all dealing with something and like society, she based her opinion of me on a visual perception.

I relate that experience to how a natural inclusion can interfere with light passing through a diamond. For example, I have the tendency to get impatient. If I had allowed that "flaw" of mine, to obstruct the light of Christ in me, she could have remained in her state of despair. A lot of times people become fixated on our flaws and prejudge us because of them. That is why it is so important for Christ's brilliance to reflect from within us, so people see more of him than they do of us. She assumed because I am physically attractive and well groomed all the time, that I have no issues. Let me be first to say; "That is farthest from the truth!"

It is amazing how people can judge us or "rate" us according to what they see. The GIA (Gemological Institute of America), rates clarity in diamonds according to grades. The ratings are on a scale of flawless to imperfect3. I have found that we can be our own worst enemy depending on how we rate or clarify ourselves. We consciously and subconsciously judge ourselves against other women's and society's standards.

For most of my younger years, I ALWAYS felt unattractive, I had low self esteem and lacked confidence. I felt this way because I was born with eczema. I never knew what it was like to have clear and smooth skin. Many summers, I endured wearing pants because my legs were scarred. In school, I had to be prepared to answer the never ending question of, "What happened to you?" I have been hospitalized and left in severe anguish due to my skin condition. Everything came to an apex when I was thirteen and all my long hair broke off from dermatitis. I was devastated and could not look at myself as being anything remotely beautiful.

I struggled to keep my issue a secret and I began to wear extensions to cover up the breakage because it was too painful to deal with. I would always envy other women with long flowing hair and smooth flawless skin.

There were many times it was unbearable and I did not want to deal with it anymore. I had a mother that tried to do everything within her power to ease my pain, but now I realize this experience of mine was and is an intricate part of my calling. I believe this is the thorn in my side. Like Paul said, in 2 Corinthians 12:8-10 (KJV), *"For this thing I besought the Lord thrice, that it might depart from me. And he said unto me, My grace is sufficient for thee: for my strength is made perfect in weakness.*

Most gladly therefore will I rather glory in my infirmities, that the power of Christ may rest upon me. Therefore I take pleasure in infirmities, in reproaches, in necessities, in persecutions, in distresses for Christ's sake: for when I am weak, then I am strong". God had to give me clarity like Paul, that in the midst of every flaw, in the midst of every issue, he would turn my weakness into his strength! It took a very long time for me to start loving myself. I would not be truthful if I did not admit that I still have some challenging moments when my eczema flares up.

To all my ladies out there dealing with sensitive physical issues,

I know what it is like to feel unattractive, to not want to look at yourself in the mirror, to not be comfortable in your own skin. It does not matter how many times someone compliments you because you only feel good for the moment. You will not believe how special you are until YOU receive it. I want you to know without a shadow of doubt that underneath that "blemish" lies something so spectacular and so luminous. God is going to use you, YES YOU! to touch the lives of many people.

We are all in fear of being judged or labeled as inferior. We all want to be accepted, but at some point I had to realize that the blemishes I had on the surface did not take away from the brilliance I possessed on the inside. What I was experiencing in the flesh did not change the beautiful clarity that God had placed inside of me. He had to show me that I carried something internally and externally beautiful and that it was precious and highly valued.

As human beings, we are always seeking acceptance by people and have a tendency to treat their opinions like the expertise of a gemologist. We allow society to judge us and determine what is beautiful aesthetically. A gemologist's rating of a diamond is naturally affected by the amount of inclusions, but we have a God that says no matter what you or others deem your flaws to be, you are still excellent, because you are made in my image!

Just as every diamond is unique and every inclusion varies in its own way, our issues are different according to how God has fashioned us. Did you know that if the flaw in a diamond does not interfere with the physical beauty of the gemstone, it is not only accepted but the flaw becomes a fascinating hallmark of authenticity that defines that gem's natural relationship with the earth?

So for all of you that think your are physically unattractive or inferior in some kind of way, I want you to know that "YOUR FLAW IS YOUR DRAW". It is what makes you distinct, it is what allows you stand out on this earth, it gives you a clarity of your own, that no one else will possess.

Even with what you consider to be your flaws, in Christ you are made whole and remember the word says in 2 Corinthians 12:9 (KJV), *"My grace is sufficient for thee, my power is made perfect in weakness"*. Nearly all diamonds and precious gems have some type of inclusion or blemish. Many of them are microscopic and can only be seen under magnification. We as individuals are blemished and flawed as well. Our internal issues can be so deeply embedded in us that they are harder to detect, but nonetheless they are there. This is why so many people seek out the help of a therapist or psychiatrist, in order to bring these hidden issues to the surface.

We have to remember, Jesus is light and the more we become Christ-like and draw towards him, our flaws and issues minimize and his light is seen through us. Just like there are ways to improve a diamond's clarity; there are ways to improve your spiritual clarity. The more clarity you possess in the spirit, the more you reflect the light of Christ. Christ said, *"As long as I am in the world, I am the light of the world"* (John 9:5 KJV).

The same applies to you. If you reflect the light of Christ, then you ultimately become the light of the world by way of him. Every time you allow the brilliance he placed in you to shine the way he has purposed, his very essence or light shines in this world. Christ gave us the Holy Spirit, as a comforter, which covers and heals us of our blemishes and inclusions. In the natural, a laser is used for laser drilling to remove dark inclusions from diamonds. The laser bores a small hole into the diamond's interior and burns away the inclusion's appearance. Another process called fracture filling, hides fractures inside of a diamond. A substance is injected into the fracture to make it less visible to improve the stone's clarity.

God uses similar techniques with us. He fills our fractures with the Holy Spirit, essentially making our worst inclusions invisible to the naked eye. He bores fine lines directly to our heart and spirit for the purpose of burning away at the flaws that we possess.

The more we draw closer to him, he draws closer to us, changing our formerly-tainted appearance to the clarity of a Christ-like appearance. Just as it says in his word, Matthew 5:16 (KJV), *"Let your light so shine before men, that they may see your good works, and glorify your Father which is in heaven"*.

The more we let our brilliance shine before the world, the more God is ultimately glorified. He injects us with his Holy Spirit which makes our former man and sinful nature less visible, virtually undetectable, and makes him more visible through us.

Carat Weight

Carat Weight is the measurement of a gem's physical weight. It is also an important factor in determining a diamond's value. Typically, the price of a diamond increases the heavier the weight of the diamond; making larger diamonds more rare and desirable. Make no mistake, two diamonds of equal carat weight can have very different values. Those values can vary depending on the clarity, color, and cut of the diamond.

When we think of the meaning of weight in the natural sense, we generally think of our physical state. As women, we can all attribute our body weight as being a sensitive issue at one time or another.
Remember, I previously mentioned that typically the heavier the diamond, the more value the diamond has. Well, how many of us have devalued ourselves because we have been overweight? Once again, we might have allowed society's depiction of a model's shape

as being more desirable than our own. The reality of this viewpoint is that we all feel the "weight" of some physical trait, that we do not particularly care for. We have to realize that our physical weight or burdens do not diminish our value.

Keep in mind, every individual's weight or burden is different, like every jewel is different. Even though some trials may appear to be similar, we have our own specific journey in life. For instance, you could have two women who have been domestically abused, but one could have been by a spouse, whereas the other could have been by a parent. One woman might not love herself because love was not expressed to her by her mother, whereas another woman might not embrace herself because her spouse is always inattentive. Am I discounting any of the pain or weight of these situations? NO, I am merely saying that everyone's experience in life is not 100% the same.

A perfect example of this point, is Pastor Christine Cain. She looks physically small in stature, but don't let the exterior appearance of this diamond fool you! I heard her preach at a women's conference and she empowered and encouraged the audience with her testimony. She may be small in the physical sense, but she is undoubtedly, a power packed diamond filled with the word of God. You have to know her testimony to understand where she gets such power.

As an adult, Pastor Christine accidently found out she was adopted. After researching her birth certificate, she found out that it did not even have her name or her parent's names listed; she was assigned a number! Can you imagine looking at your birth certificate and finding out that you did not even have a name?

She was raised by her adoptive parents in a high crime and drug infested housing project in Australia. Being molested by family members since the age of 12, she had more reasons than most to completely give up, but school became her outlet. She became the only person in her graduating class to go on to college.

Pastor Christine eventually met her future husband and was blessed with a beautiful family. She became a leader at the world renowned Hillsong Church, in addition to starting ministries of her own. She ultimately had to realize she had value even in the midst of the weight she had to carry. As discomforting as it may seem, it is the experiences in our lives that help to strengthen us and define who we really are. A lot of times we go through situations that should have destroyed us. Some of us have experienced divorce, loss of a child, or possibly a life changing illness. Any one of those situations is enough to make one feel that life is just too much to bear.

My beautiful gems, I need you to realize that you were made to carry the weight of your experiences. I want you to write on a piece of paper, "I WAS MADE TO CARRY THE WEIGHT". The next time you are feeling overwhelmed by your situation, I want you to look at that paper and repeat those words until you receive them in your spirit.

Keep in mind, when a diamond is first mined, it is rough, jagged and oversized. It is not until it has been cut that the true carat weight is determined. So know that through your trials, you will processed to carry the weight of your situation. Even though it does not feel like it, trust me when I tell you... YOU WILL SURVIVE. God's word says, in Psalm 118:17 (KJV), *"I shall not die, but live, and declare the works of the Lord"*. Just like Pastor Christine, God has a specific plan for your life that he will bring to pass.

I know you are probably saying, "This author has not walked in my footsteps, she has no idea what I have been through". Well your right, I may not know your situation, but I do know WE are made in God's image. It means... WE both have the same God, and OUR God knows the thoughts that he thinks towards us, thoughts of peace and not evil, to give us an expected end (Jeremiah 29:11 KJV).

It is never his desire to hurt us or watch us suffer, but remember, even a diamond goes through a strenuous process to be formed. I can still feel some of you saying, "My situation is too much to bear, or this crisis is too much to endure". Jesus had the weight of the world on his shoulders. At one point, even the powerful Son of God asked the Father that this cup be taken from him. In the end, he was willing to bear the weight of our sins, so we could have everlasting life.

He ultimately told his father, *"Nevertheless not my will, but thine, be done"* (Luke 22:42 KJV). He carried the weight until the very end and what he received afterwards was far worth it! By carrying the burden of your experience, you will receive the benefits of everlasting life, a constant way of escape, strength in weakness, legions of angels to your rescue, and mountains moved by way of your speech... but most of all your name, written in the Lamb's Book of Life!

The most amazing thing of all is that Jesus knew how hard the circumstances in our lives would be. He knew how weary we would become. He knew how hard it would be to carry the burdens of this world, because he ultimately went through it first. Jesus was talked about, persecuted, beat, lied on, and cast out. He was crushed by the "weight" of sin in order to become the propitiation of sin for us. He was submerged in the harshest conditions that this world could offer.

Because Jesus loves us so much, he left us the Holy Spirit. As his people, he knew that we would endure the same hardships and trials as him. We all have been persecuted and treated unjustly in some way or another in our lives. I relate the Holy Spirit to the prongs that are wrapped around a diamond. They are there to hold it in place and keep it secure. Jesus left us the Holy Spirit to keep us secure. I can recall hitting my ring against a table and nervously I looked down, only to see the diamond was still in place and undamaged.

Well, that is the Holy Spirit in our lives, it keeps us firmly planted in the midst of life's storms. Just like Jesus took the weight for us, the Holy Spirit helps us carry the weight of our walk. We might get tossed about, shook up from time to time by the storms of life, but in the end we come out standing strong!

I can recall so many times in my life that I did not think I was going to make it. My husband and I moved into our new home and within 6 months he was laid off by his employer. We did not know what we were going to do, but we believed God would bring us through. I had shortly thereafter started my business, so that was a big help financially. We assumed this setback was only temporary, so we were not overly worried. Needless to say, we endured this season for 4 YEARS.

Just when we thought things could not get any worse, they did. With 2 small children, we struggled to maintain daily life as we knew it. I was working as many hours as I could promoting my business, but it was not enough. Now, I am used to maintaining a pretty decent lifestyle, so if I saw something I wanted, I had the means to get it. As time progressed, even that comfort slowly disappeared.

The simple things, that a woman looks forward to, like getting my hair and nails professionally done, GONE (might I add that I have always prided myself on keeping up with my appearance, so that was a hard pill to swallow). Going out to eat occasionally, GONE, Being able to get basic necessities from time to time, GONE. Paying the mortgage, much less the basic utilities was an immense struggle. There were days we truly did not know how we were going to survive.

During this entire time, God would send those we least expected, (his team of angels) to bless us and open up business opportunities. He sought to make diamonds of us. God was moving away enough earth to leave an inclusion or a carbon spot in our lives. It was just enough to provide us with a glorious testimony during our journey, but it still wasn't time to be unearthed yet... because we had some more weight to bear. I remember sitting in my living room, balled up on the floor and crying out to God. I said, " I know I can handle a lot Lord, but this is too much, I can't take it... I just can't take it". I felt like a failure as a entrepreneur, as a mother, even as a woman. I had to lean on God and his word more than ever, his word that says, *"And God is faithful; he will not let you be tempted beyond what you can bear, But when you are tempted, he will also provide a way out so that you can endure"* (1Cor 10:13 KJV). God continued to show me that HE, being the great "I AM" was covering us. He was our way out, our "prongs" so to speak. He showed us that all we had to do was stay fixated on him and he would hold us up and keep us strong during that season. Time and time again, God did just that.

When thousands of people's unemployment benefits were not processed, my husband's benefits were processed (to the amazement of the agency employees). My husband practically had a job handed to him during a season when thousands were struggling to gain employment. More business opportunities came our way and we were blessed with a free car from our neighbor. Our list of blessings are too many to name, but God showed us in this season, that all we needed was him to hold us up.

God truly was "our prongs". His hands were perfectly molded around us to hold us up and carry us through our circumstances. Truly believing in him and hearing from the Holy Spirit were the only things that kept us going. He had to show me that I could make it. He had to show me that I could take it. God showed me that I was a treasured diamond in his sight. He made me feel like a valuable gem when he came to my aid time and time again. He caused men to give in our lives, in a way that was unimaginable in the world's eyes!

God allowed me to go through, just like his son in order to bring me to a greater place. I realized that I didn't need all of the vices and comforts that I thought I needed. I became more humbled, I became wiser and I matured spiritually. He had me carry my cross, carry my weight, in order to be crucified, to become even more brilliant than I ever knew I could be. Like Jesus, each lash I sustained through my experiences added to my weight, making me heavy. When I allowed myself to be nailed to the cross and to surrender to the Holy Spirit, the weight of my trial became lighter.

Typically, the heavier a diamond gets, the more value it possesses. Only through trials and tribulations can one find out what they are truly made of. God wants you to see that when you go through your trial, HE will be the prong that keeps you strong enough to carry the weight.

I mention in the next chapter, that garnets are found to have the same specific gravity of diamonds. Can you guess the specific difference between the two gemstones outside of their color? Garnets fracture more easily and drift with the sand, whereas diamonds move with the heavier rocks. You are not a garnet, YOU ARE A DIAMOND!

God had to show me that I would not fracture easily. I was a diamond built to carry the heavy weight of my situation and so are you!

Copy Cat

We have officially touched on all of the 4 C's; Color, Cut, Clarity, and Carat weight. In discussing these factors, we see how each of them attribute to the radiance of the gem and ourselves. Now that we have discovered the roots our radiant spirit, I want you to ask yourself, Are you reflecting your own brilliance or the brilliance of someone else? It is a good question, because we never stop to think whether what we display is our own uniqueness or a simulation of someone else.

As with natural diamonds, given their rarity and value, it is not surprising that someone would seek to enhance or replicate their beauty. Gemologists state that in recent years, diamond treatments, simulated diamonds, and synthetic diamonds have become more common. In light of these developments, authentic diamonds have become harder to detect. Believe it or not, this point relates to us in the natural also. As an author, your thoughts might be: Why should I write a book about success? There are 10 million books on the market about success already. My word to you: Don't let that discourage you. We are in an era where there are many authors, coaches, motivational speakers and other professions, but know that you have something specific and special placed inside of you to bring to the table.

There might be many authors alongside of you, but none of them can tell your story and other speakers can't motivate according to the way YOU are fashioned. Always remember, a synthetic diamond is man-made as a result of a technological process unlike a natural diamond that is the result of a geographical process. They might appear to look the same on the surface, but the process of how they are created is different. Now, don't get me wrong, we are all influenced by other people. Mentors, media, public figures, celebrities, and other role models play a part in developing our persona.

We have to keep in mind, that God created us in a specific way unlike anyone else. So you can't expect your story to sound like someone else's story and others can't tell your story with the same passion you would, because they did not experience your circumstances.

It is so easy for us to desire the brilliance in someone else yet not see the brilliance in ourselves. Because of that desire, we start to simulate what we see in other people. We simulate their speech patterns, mannerisms, and other behaviors, looking for the same impartation of brilliance on our life. I equate it to fashion. If I see you in a outfit, buy that outfit and put it on, I will not look like you, because I am not you.

I can't take your radiance, make it mine and vice versa. You say imitation is the sincerest form of flattery, yes it is, but your brilliance will never be seen if you are shadowing someone else. You ultimately take on the nature of a simulated diamond, when you attempt to flow fully in someone else's brilliance; instead of reflecting your own unique spirit.

Actually, we do this more often than not, but then can't understand why we are not experiencing the same level of success as the person that we are imitating. I recall a time when my business growth was stagnant. I was trying to find ways to improve my business and take it to the next level. I tried to implement a business model that was used by someone else, to no avail, it did not really work for me.

There were some points of value, but all of it was not meant for me to adopt. The principle that applies here, is that the information was good to tweak and enhance my business model, but not to completely alter it.

When we begin to simulate someone else's persona, we lose sight of our own individuality and uniqueness. Have you ever heard two singers that sound alike? or have you seen an actress and said "She performs just like the actress from that movie". They were possibly mistaken for someone else because they adopted a large part of that actor's persona. The recognition they received was not for their brilliance but for someone else's.

At first thought, it might have been hard for you to detect who the actual actor was, but with a little thought you figured it out. Take note, a cubic zirconia might look like a diamond, but it can never possess the same qualities and value that a real diamond has. It gives the appeal of the real thing to compliment and satisfy one's desires, but no matter how convincing the "illusion", its true characteristics can be identified by a trained gemologist. Just like the testing from a gemologist can identify a simulant, the testing from the Holy Spirit can identify when someone is an imitation.

As I began my research for this book, I found out when miners are looking for diamond sources, there are other stones that generally indicate that diamonds are nearby. When miners come across purple garnets, it is a good indicator that diamonds are present. Locating garnets are often key to finding diamonds. Diamond prospectors state that diamonds and garnets have nearly the same specific gravity. The big difference between the two gems is garnets fracture more easily and drift away with the sand, whereas diamonds move with the heavier rocks.

There might be someone that is drawn to you, even trying to imitate you or take credit for something you have implemented. When everything is said and done, the original, the "true" representation, is the one that remains in the end.

God's word says, in Luke 8:17 (KJV), *"For nothing is secret, that shall not be made manifest; neither anything hid, that shall not be known and come abroad"*. Remember, God will always allow the truth to be revealed.

Lets recall the story about the sons of Sceva in the bible. They attempted to cast out demons in Jesus' name only to be called out by the demons. The sons of Sceva were "simulating" the disciples to act out healing and casting out devils in Jesus' name.

The scripture reads (Acts 19:13-16 KJV):
"There were certain exorcists, vagabond Jews took upon them to call over them which had evil spirits the name of the Lord Jesus saying, "We adjure you by Jesus whom Paul preacheth". And there were seven of one Sceva, a Jew and the chief of the priests, which did so. And the evil spirit answered and said, "Jesus I know, and Paul I know; but who are ye?" And the man in whom the evil spirit was

leaped on them, and overcame them, and prevailed against them, so that they fled out of that house naked and wounded". The demon recognized that the sons of Sceva did not have the same power as the disciples or Jesus. They were trying to imitate the very power they did not possess

When I think of the sons of Sceva, I relate them to the simulations and synthetic diamonds that have become so common in the marketplace. In the chapter, Color, I discussed enhancements such as coating, which enhances a diamond's color, in order to mask an undesirable body color within a diamond. I also mentioned, HPHT, which is a process that actually changes the color of the diamond, making it colorless (a colorless state improves the value of the diamond) and virtually undetectable.

Other popular practices such as laser drilling and fracture filling are used to remove dark flaws and hide fractures within a diamond. These are perfect examples how something or someone can appear to be other than what they really are. A faux diamond can be detected as well as a person trying to utilize power or talent they do not possess.

It is the same way in the world and the body of Christ, as it is with diamonds. We have more people than ever before trying to replicate and even steal another person's brilliance and anointing. Because we have a God that stands for truth, they will always be exposed. A very important point to remember is...the anointing CAN NOT be faked! It is something precious, bestowed solely from God. People might be fooled for a while, but eventually they will be able to tell when you are riding off of someone else's brilliance and not your own. They can tell when a synthetic diamond is being displayed versus the real thing.

You also have to be very careful, when you take on certain attributes of other people, because you can affect the value of the preciousness that God placed inside of you. You might not feel it in your spirit or see it in yourself, but Psalm 139:14 (KJV) reads, *"I will praise you, for I am fearfully and wonderfully made; marvelous are your works, and my soul knows very well"*. When God created you, you were made marvelously, he made you in a fearful and wonderful fashion, like no other. If you opt to deny the preciousness he has placed in you, it is like saying he has made a mistake.

We know we have a creator that makes everything perfect in his image. You will never have the level of gratification or success trying to operate in someone else's brilliance. Not only will you miss out on your blessing, but there will be people you were specifically called to connect with that will miss out on their blessing as well. Remember no two diamonds are created exactly alike, so be the diamond **YOU** were created to be.

Care

Even though you have the durability of a diamond, you are not completely indestructible. Diamonds can be chipped by a sharp blow or become loose from a weakened setting. In the same manner you would care for a jewel, you have to make it a priority to protect your God given brilliance at all cost. You have to stay saturated in God's word and the word he has spoken over your life or you could possibly lose your radiance.

You have to be around others with precious like faith and you can't allow your prongs to become loose or your connection with the Holy Spirit to be weakened. You need to stay firmly planted in who and what God has called you to be. Gemologists recommend that when caring for precious gems, stones of equal hardness should be stored together. Why the importance, you ask? To prevent harder stones from scratching softer stones. This point is comparable to the scripture 2 Corinthians 6:14 (KJV), *"Be ye not unequally yoked together with unbelievers: for what fellowship hath righteousness with unrighteousness? and what communion hath light with darkness?"*. You do not want your brilliance tainted or marred by others of unlike faith. Light can be dimmed by darkness but can shine even brighter with more light!

It is important for a diamond to be secure in its setting (prongs), or it can loosen and fall out. Being a person of brilliance, you have to make sure you are secure in who you are, because you can lose your true identity to worldly devices. Make sure you use your gift of perception or discernment to guard yourself from any deception the world sends your way. The deception and trickery that comes to diminish your brilliance and have you believe you are not who God called you to be.

Since we know that diamonds can be damaged, you must guard yourselves from the wolves in sheep's clothing. The people that appear to be for you but are actually against you; those who take joy in you straying off the path to your destiny.

In the story of David, Saul knew the greatness that David possessed. He knew what destiny awaited him. Saul kept him close not out of love, but to keep a watchful eye over him. He envied David's greatness and knew he would one day be king. King Saul also used David's superiority as a warrior to defeat his enemies. He used David's brilliance for his benefit while also desiring the warrior's downfall.

You have to be cautious, not just of other people, but your own desires as well. In James 1:14 (KJV), it says, *"But every man is tempted, when he is drawn away of his own lust and enticed"*. Sometimes it is not others that want to steal our brilliance, but we ourselves that misuse it. Have you ever used your God given gift in a manner not befitting to God? Or used your God given radiance solely for your own vain glory? The word says in Romans 11:29 (KJV), *"For the gifts and calling of God are given without repentance"*. All gifts and talents bestowed upon us are from him, even though we may not be using them in a way that honors him.

Don't feel bad if you have experienced that scenario. We have all had moments where we have fallen short due to our goals and aspirations.

I remember receiving an opportunity for my first major preaching engagement. I was so excited. I started contemplating how much I was going to charge and the exposure I would get from it. Needless to say, the negotiations fell apart and it did not happen.

God revealed to me that I can't put a price on a word that HE gave me. Now I am sure, I have rattled some cages here, HE explained that this was not my business, Divacoutoure. This is HIS ministry and HIS brilliance that HE gave me to impact HIS people. He was not going to allow me to sell my anointing, or rather HIS anointing (because he placed it inside of me) for my own glory. So we have to always be careful and conscious of what our motives are when it comes to the brilliance that he has placed inside of us.

Just like there is an attraction to the anointing on your life, there is definitely an attraction to the radiance of a diamond. If you have ever seen what you consider to be the perfect diamond in a showcase, you know exactly what I am talking about. Its brilliance and shine just draws you to the point where you want to try it on. Some people are attracted to your brilliance to the point where they will covet you. For this and many other reasons, you have to be leery who you entertain and connect with. You have to protect your brilliance at all cost. Certain people will see the anointing you possess and draw on you to the point you become drained and lose your luster.

The word tells us that, *"The enemy comes to steal, kill and destroy"* (John 10:10 KJV). People will latch onto you to steal your anointing and even kill for it. Diamonds, have been sought after and killed for due to the value they possess, so why would people not think twice to destroy you for what you possess in the natural and in the spirit?

It is so important to know who you are and what you possess. When you don't know what you possess, one of two things could possibly happen: 1. People in spiritual leadership or authoritative positions will not share the revelation of who you are with you, leaving you stifled in the spirit and in the natural or 2. They *will* share it and tap into your talents for their benefit. You have to know who you are in Christ to first embrace yourself and only then will you know how others should care for you.

Before I really embraced who I was, I had few experiences where others were able to take advantage of me and hinder my spiritual growth. For many years in my spiritual journey, I did not have any guidance and was left to find my own way. I was given the notion that I was being taken under someone's wing to be spiritually mentored. However, I quickly realized, that it was not with the intention to help me spiritually, only to benefit from the talents that I possessed.

There are people that only desire to use you for the expertise you possess in the natural to benefit them. I thank God that I knew who I was in Christ and what I possessed. My previous ministry experience could have left me feeling like I was "second best" or only worth the validation that others would occasionally give me. Have you ever connected with people that made you feel like *they* were doing you a favor by utilizing you for your expertise? Well, that was me!

Pointing out the story of David again, he was the youngest of twelve and did not have the most brawn among his siblings. He was only a shepherd boy, but was the one destined to be a great warrior and king. Even when he did not have the title of King, he was treasured in God's eyes. That is why it so imperative to know your value. If society never gives you a title or never gives you an accolade, know that you are priceless.

Even a diamond in its raw state is still priceless. Just because it has not been rated does not mean it is not valuable. Like David, I was overlooked and not taken seriously. I was told I was anointed, had many gifts and talents, but was barely called upon.

I have been in a ministry, that as soon as they realized my family and I were not in league with "their program", we were shunned. I gave my life to Christ when I was 28 years old and went many years without real spiritual guidance. Feeling lost with no sense of purpose, God had to reveal to me who I was, a rare gem. He had to show me that the previous ministries I was at, could not unearth the brilliance inside of me.

God sent people into my life at the right time. People who confirmed what he had spoken over my life and made sure I was guided into my purpose the right way. God had to reveal to me that even if man does not confirm me publicly, I would not be denied of who God had called and confirmed me to be. His word says in Jeremiah 5:1 (NIV), *"I knew you before I formed you in your mother's womb. Before you were born I set you apart and appointed you as my spokesman to the world"*. So no matter what plan man has devised to deny you, know that you have been set aside and appointed by God!

A lot people see the brilliance you possess and out of envy and jealously will not reveal it to you. They would rather keep you stuck, hindering you from being all that God has called you to be, while they continue to grow. In John 14:6 (KJV), it says, *"Jesus saith unto him, I am the way, the truth, and the life: no man cometh unto the Father, but by me"*. Once the truth is revealed, once you allow the light of Christ to shine brilliantly through you, and you know who the father has created you to be... YOU CAN NO LONGER BE DENIED! A diamond radiates and draws all attention unto it, just like the brilliance that God has placed inside of you.

Closure

God's ultimate plan is to purify us and make us whole, by using our brilliance for his glory. When a diamond is originally created it is only a piece of dark carbon. As the diamond is cut and goes through its process, it becomes pure enough for its true brilliance to be seen. God does the same with us. When we were created we were shaped in iniquity which is ultimately darkness. When we go through our process, we are tried and proven, and then his light shines ever so brightly through us!

Jesus is the perfect diamond, cut to perfection and flawless in God's eyes. It was God who said, in Matthew 3:17 (KJV), *"This is my beloved son, in whom I am well pleased"*. The more that Christ's brilliance inside of us is shown, the more God is pleased with us as well! A diamond represents strength, endurance, pureness, and light...

all things that reflect God. All things that you will represent when you have been tried and proven through your process.

Know that just like each finished diamond is a unique stone fashioned by its cutter, you are a unique and one of a kind vessel created by God! You have been fashioned, cut, and polished a particular way unlike anyone else. You should no longer wonder why you never fit in; it was because you were made to stand out. Like a diamond... YOU ARE RARE!

It is no mistake that people are attracted to diamonds far more than any other gemstone. Familiar spirits are attracted to one another, brilliance is drawn to brilliance and both possess precious like qualities. But there are spirits in play that camouflage themselves in order to hinder you from shining bright and becoming everything that God has called you to be.

You have to be cautious of the enemy. He wishes to block and hide your brilliance. The devil was once beautiful and brilliant himself, so he is a master of trickery. If he can get you to use your brilliance for your fleshly desires, HE HAS WON! If he can get his legions of followers to drain you dry of your preciousness, HE HAS WON! If he can hinder you from ever realizing the brilliance you possess, HE HAS WON! He is no longer precious in God's eyes. He no longer represents beauty and light, but represents darkness. So he wants you to stay in the dark and hidden from the destiny that awaits you.

Find out the brilliance you possess and guard it all cost. The enemy would love to have you believe you are not equipped enough, you are not beautiful enough, and you have been through so much that you will not make it. But I am here to tell you, that YOU WILL MAKE IT! He told me the same lie. He told me because I did not have a title given by man, that I was not usable. But how many of you know that God created us and God is the ONLY ONE that needs to validate us. Like a precious diamond, he has given us top rating!

It is the enemy's desire for you to never know how precious you are, for you to stay in your raw state, for you to stay in darkness along with him. He used to be a precious gem in God's eyes. Ezekiel 28:13 (KJV) states, *"Thou hast been in Eden the garden of God; every precious stone was thy covering, the sardius, topaz, and the diamond, the beryl, the onyx, and the jasper, the sapphire, the emerald..."* He was God's precious jewel and because of his iniquity, he was cast out of heaven into darkness. He would love nothing more than for you to join him. He knows if you ever yield to God and allow him to take you through your process, you will be strong and unconquerable like a diamond.

The same way God strategically used certain colored jewels, to build the 12 foundations in the city of New Jerusalem, he wants to use you in your precious-like state to build his kingdom. YOU ARE THE CONDUIT! YOU ARE THE ONE! He will use you in appointed places and at appointed times that he can't use anyone else. That makes you rare, that makes you precious, that makes you a diamond.

I have come to the realization, that the hardest part of the battle called life is loving ourselves. We find it easier to display love to our children, spouses, and friends. The deception in that mindset is you can't truly love yourself or anyone else without receiving God's love first. God brings divine people in our lives who have been touched by him to show us true love. When we receive true love, then we come to know HIS love. Only then, are we in a position to be a vessel for his love and his light to be passed on to others.

Another profound revelation is that a wedding ring, naturally symbolizes a never ending covenant between man and woman unto God. The bible states in 1 John 4:8 (KJV), that *God is love*! Everything about a diamond represents love, brilliance, endurance, light, and purity; all attributes of Christ, who was the ultimate jewel. If you are brethren of Christ then you are jewel unto God also!

It is amazing that the diamond has become the gift of love and Jesus' final instruction in the New Testament, was *to love one another, as he has loved us, so all men will know that we are his disciples if we love one another* (John 13:33-35 KJV). The basis of our walk in this world is to love and by showing love, Jesus is revealed and God gets the glory.

I hope you now see how precious you really are and how valuable the brilliance is that lies inside of you. I can't stress enough the importance of being wary of who you connect and collaborate with.

There are people who envy and desire what you have. They will drain your anointing and talents at the expense of their own agenda.

For those that still question their value, I say YOU ARE PRECIOUS AND YOU CAN DO THIS! You have to believe that God was doing a great work when he created you. He does not make mistakes and you are equipped to do everything that he has called you to do. His word states, in 1 John 4:4 (KJV), that *"Greater is he that is in you, than he that is in the world"*. With the Holy Spirit being the "prongs" that keep your brilliance secure, you can carry the weight and complete any task that comes your way.

I want you to know that GOD LOVES YOU SO MUCH! The fact that he created you, the fact that he sacrificed his son for you, the fact that he placed so many brilliant qualities inside of you are only a few amazing reasons.

His desire is to journey with you as his precious jewel and ultimately say to you, *"My daughter, in whom I am well pleased"*.

It is time for you to awake, it is time for you to come forth, it is time for you to walk the earth in the boldness of the stunning gem that you are! You have been hidden from the world long enough. You were behind, you were beneath, but like a diamond, you just went through your process and catapulted to the surface! The same way Jesus ascended into glory, you have now ascended to reveal your greatness to the world for God's glory.

Through him I was cut, Through him I was created to carry the weight. Through him I was made whole by the absence of my own color. Through me the clarity of him is revealed. Through him... I was made a DIAMOND, and so shall you!

Scriptures

May the referenced scriptures uplift and encourage you daily. You can make it through any challenge... YOU ARE A DIAMOND!

2 Corinthians 1:5 - "For as the sufferings of Christ abound in us, so our consolation also aboundeth by Christ".

Isaiah 64:8 - "But now, O Lord, thou art our father, we are the clay, and thou our potter, and we all are the work of thy hand".

Luke 22:42 - "Nevertheless, not my will, but thine, be done".

James 1:2-4 - "Consider it pure joy, my brothers and sisters, whenever you face trials of many kinds, because you know that the testing of your faith produces perseverance. Let perseverance finish its work so that you may be mature and complete, not lacking anything".

2 Corinthians 12:8-10 - " For this thing I besought the Lord thrice, that it might depart from me. And he said unto me, My grace is sufficient for thee: for my strength is made perfect in weakness".

John 9:5 - "As long as I am in the world, I am the light of the world".

Matthew 5:16 - "Let your light so shine before men, that they may see your good works, and glorify your Father which is in heaven".

Psalm 118:17 - "I shall not die, but live, and declare the works of the Lord".

Jeremiah 29:11 - "He knows the thoughts that he thinks towards us, thoughts of peace and not evil, to give us an expected end".

1 Corinthians 10:13 - "And God is faithful; he will not let you be tempted beyond what you can bear, But when you are tempted, he will also provide a way out so that you can endure".

Luke 8:17 - "For nothing is secret, that shall not be made manifest; neither anything hid, that shall not be known and come abroad".

Psalms 139:14 - "I will praise you, for I am fearfully and wonderfully made; marvelous are your works, and my soul knows very well".

2 Corinthians 6:14 - "Be ye not unequally yoked together with unbelievers".

James 1:14 - "But every man is tempted, when he is drawn away of his own lust and enticed".

Romans 11:29 - "For the gifts and calling of God are given without repentance".

John 10:10 - "The enemy comes to steal, kill and destroy".

Jeremiah 5:1 - "I knew you before I formed you in your mother's womb. Before you were born I set you apart and appointed you as my spokesman to the world".

John 14:6 - "Jesus saith unto him, I am the way, the truth, and the life: no man cometh unto the Father, but by me".

Matthew 3:17 - "This is my beloved son, in whom I am well pleased".

1 John 4:8 - " He that loveth not knoweth not God; for God is love".

John 13:35 - "Love one another, as he has loved us, so all men will know that we are his disciples if we love one another".

1 John 4:4 - "Greater is he that is in you, than he that is in the world".

About the Author

Dell Scott, also known as "Diva Dell", is the CEO of Divacoutoure. As a speaker, she ministers with the strong desire to see women become empowered by unleashing their inner brilliance. Dell's purpose and passion is to show women how to believe in themselves and realize that they are made in excellence. She reveals to women the importance of image in order to succeed in their personal lives as well as their career. With a calling, to also impact women at a younger age, Dell utilizes her skill set to mentor the youth in local forums.

As the visionary and creative force of Divacoutoure, it is her company's mission to see women become empowered to unleash their "Inner Diva" through the art of exquisite fashion. Divacoutoure is a "Tour de Fashion" boutique with various fashion retail products and services.

Being a Designer and Fashion Stylist, Dell shows women how to transcend their inner beauty to the outside for all to see. She finds joy in seeing women further enhance the beauty they already possess.

As an Author, Dell expressed the challenges of being a kingdom wife, mother, and entrepreneur. This message was brought to the world in her co-authored," MRS. BOSS, Vol 1: Memoirs of Divas that Hold it Down Fearlessly". Her new release, "The Undiscovered Jewel, Realizing the Brilliance That Lies Within", taps into the revelation that women need to know that they are precious and brilliant in order to reveal their "true selves" to the world. She is the fashion columnist for K.I.S.H. magazine and currently authors the fashion newsletter, Fab Factor.

Dell resides in Clayton, DE. with her husband Jermaine and two children, Jasmin and Jermaine II.

Contact:

Speaking engagements:
www.dellscott.com
info@dellscott.com
1-800-804-0194/Ext. 6

Fashion retail products and services:
www.divacoutoure.com
info@divacoutoure.com
1-800-804-0194

Sources

Gemological Institute of America Inc. 4C's Education, 2002-2012. Web.

"Bible Precious Stones." McdonoughInfo.com, Durable Riches in the Endtimes, Web. n.p. n.d.

Hayes, Jeffrey. "Looking For and Mining Diamonds." Factsanddetails.com, Web. 2009, updated 2011 March.

"Meanings of Gemstones." Hubpages, Estranged 911, Web. 24 June. 2011.

"List of precious stones in the bible.", Wikipedia, n.p., n.a. Web. 14 February. 2014.

"New Jerusalem.", Wikipedia, n.p., n.a. Web. 14 January. 2014
"Diamond Information." Jewelsmiths.com, n.p., n.d., Web.

"Jewel", Freedictionary.com, Farlex, n.d. Web.

The Holy Bible, NIV. Biblegateway.com, Zondervan Corporation, L.L.C., 2010 Web.

The Holy Bible, KJV. Biblegateway.com, Zondervan Corporation, L.L.C., 2010 Web.

Additional copies of this book and other books from Dell Scott are available at www.dellscott.com

EMAIL US YOUR STORY!

Please give Dell the privilege of hearing how the message of "The Undiscovered Jewel" has impacted you or a loved one. Email at: info@undiscoveredjewel.com or Post a comment at www.facebook.com/theundiscoveredjewel.

THREEFOLD PUBLISHING

WWW.THREEFOLDPUBLISHING.COM

To all my of my beautiful gems......

Receive...Believe...Acheive!

ISBN 978-1-63068-696-3